50 Quick Ways to

Perfect Behaviour
Management

By Mike Gershon

About the Author

Mike Gershon is a teacher, trainer and writer. He is the author of twenty books on teaching, learning and education, including a number of bestsellers, as well as the co-author of one other. Mike's online resources have been viewed and downloaded more than 2.5 million times by teachers in over 180 countries and territories. He is a regular contributor to the Times Educational Supplement and has created a series of electronic CPD guides for TES PRO. Find out more, get in touch and download free resources at www.mikegershon.com

Training and Consultancy

Mike is an expert trainer whose sessions have received acclaim from teachers across England. Recent bookings include:

- *Improving Literacy Levels in Every Classroom*, St Leonard's Academy, Sussex

- *Growth Mindsets, Effective Marking and Feedback* Ash Manor School, Aldershot

- *Effective Differentiation,* Tri-Borough Alternative Provision (TBAP), London

Mike also works as a consultant, advising on teaching and learning and creating bespoke materials for schools. Recent work includes:

- *Developing and Facilitating Independent Learning,* Chipping Norton School, Oxfordshire

- *Differentiation In-Service Training,* Charles Darwin School, Kent

If you would like speak to Mike about the services he can offer your school, please get in touch by email: mike@mikegershon.com

Other Works from the Same Authors

Available to buy now on Amazon:

How to use Differentiation in the Classroom: The Complete Guide

How to use Assessment for Learning in the Classroom: The Complete Guide

How to use Questioning in the Classroom: The Complete Guide

How to use Discussion in the Classroom: The Complete Guide

How to Teach EAL Students in the Classroom: The Complete Guide

More Secondary Starters and Plenaries

Secondary Starters and Plenaries: History

Teach Now! History: Becoming a Great History Teacher

The Growth Mindset Pocketbook (with Professor Barry Hymer)

How to be Outstanding in the Classroom

Also available to buy now on Amazon, the entire 'Quick 50' Series:

50 Quick and Brilliant Teaching Ideas

50 Quick and Brilliant Teaching Techniques

50 Quick and Easy Lesson Activities

50 Quick Ways to Help Your Students Secure A and B Grades at GCSE

50 Quick Ways to Help Your Students Think, Learn, and Use Their Brains Brilliantly

50 Quick Ways to Motivate and Engage Your Students

50 Quick Ways to Outstanding Teaching

50 Quick Ways to Perfect Behaviour Management

50 Quick and Brilliant Teaching Games

50 Quick and Easy Ways to Outstanding Group Work

50 Quick and Easy Ways to Prepare for Ofsted

50 Quick and Easy Ways Leaders can Prepare for Ofsted

About the Series

The 'Quick 50' series was born out of a desire to provide teachers with practical, tried and tested ideas, activities, strategies and techniques which would help them to teach brilliant lessons, raise achievement and engage and inspire their students.

Every title in the series distils great teaching wisdom into fifty bite-sized chunks. These are easy to digest and easy to apply – perfect for the busy teacher who wants to develop their practice and support their students.

Acknowledgements

As ever I must thank all the fantastic colleagues and students I have worked with over the years, first while training at the Institute of Education, Central Foundation Girls' School and Nower Hill High School and subsequently while working at Pimlico Academy and King Edward VI School in Bury St Edmunds.

Thanks also to Alison and Andrew Metcalfe for a great place to write and finally to Gordon at KallKwik for help with the covers.

Table of Contents

Introduction

Decide What You Want

Set Your Boundaries

Work Out Your Responses

Communicate Your Boundaries

Communicate Your Consequences

Police Your Boundaries

Always Follow Through on Your Consequences

Don't Fold

Short-Term Pain = Long-Term Gain

Be Consistent. Always.

Radiate Enthusiasm

Keep Positive

Praise

Praise Spotting

Genuine Praise

Specific Praise

Praise Effort, Application and Persistence

Written Praise

Spoken Praise

Non-Verbal Praise

Plan Great Lessons

Keep It Challenging

Find Ways to Ensure Success

Especially at the Start

Ask Yourself What the Students Will Be Doing

Personalise the Learning

Make it Relevant

If You're Bored, They're Bored

But Sometimes We Need to be Bored

Give and You Shall Receive

We All Like Something to Look Forward To

Manners All Round

Model, Model, Model

Never Speak if They're Speaking

Don't be Afraid to Wait

Remain Flexible

Sense the Atmosphere

Focus on the Small Things

But Don't Get Pedantic

High Standards

Lock-Down Lessons

Use Your Seating Plan

Say 'Thanks'

Take Control

Organisation is Key

Use Your Voice

Use Your Body

Never Break a Silence

Do Your Research

Stay Calm

A Brief Request

Introduction

Welcome to '50 Quick Ways to Perfect Behaviour Management.'

This book is all about the practical things you can do in the classroom to make sure behaviour in your lessons is always of the highest standard; focussed on learning; respectful; and the cornerstone of outstanding teaching.

Every entry presents a different idea, strategy or technique. Some of these are connected. Some stand alone. All will help you to manage behaviour brilliantly. All will help you to get the very best out of your students so that you can unlock their potential and create a fantastic atmosphere for learning.

So read on and enjoy! The book stems from my own experience as a teacher and trainer. I hope it gives you everything you need to have perfect behaviour management every time you teach.

Decide What You Want

01 When undertaking any enterprise it is important to begin by deciding what you want to get out of it.

You are a teacher.

Your enterprise is teaching.

You need to decide what you want your classroom to be like. How will students act? What will they do? How will learning happen?

Before we begin examining different behaviour management strategies and techniques, spend some time asking yourself what you want.

Having a final goal in mind will give you something to focus on. It will act as a lens through which to refine everything you do. And it will give you a means by which to judge when whether you have achieved your aims (which, with the help of this book, should hopefully be fairly soon!).

Set Your Boundaries

02 In every area of life there are rules. Mostly these are unwritten. They are the norms we follow. In Britain, to take one example, an unwritten rule states that you should say please and thank you when interacting with others. Not everyone follows this rule but the rule is there nonetheless.

Similarly, when you talk with a friend you understand the rules governing your conversation: turn-taking; specific use of language; expectation of sympathy; shared history; and shared assumptions.

The classroom is the same as every other area of life. It has unwritten rules which regulate behaviour.

Perfect behaviour management requires you to take charge of these rules from the word go. You need to set your boundaries as soon as possible so that pupils know what you expect of them. You then need to reinforce these boundaries rigorously. This way, students will come to see that they are fixed and that you are in charge.

Ultimately, it is about you shaping the atmosphere of your classroom.

Work Out Your Responses

03 We must accept as inevitable the fact that students will overstep the boundaries we set.

This is natural.

It's part of growing up.

Children and young adults test boundaries in order to find out how far they can go. It is not something that is unusual and nor should you see it as a necessarily bad thing in and of itself. After all, it is through testing boundaries that pupils come to realise what is and isn't acceptable.

Bearing this in mind, work out in advance how you will respond to boundaries being overstepped.

This way, you will never be caught out. You will always have a response ready, allowing you to deal swiftly and calmly with any behaviour you do not deem acceptable.

Communicate Your Boundaries

04 A frequent failing when it comes to behaviour management is ambiguity. This is something we are all guilty of from time to time.

Ambiguity makes life harder for students than it needs to be. They find themselves uncertain about what is acceptable, what responses are likely to be forthcoming and what it is that you want them to do.

Clearly communicating your boundaries will ensure there is absolutely no ambiguity over what is and what isn't acceptable.

This will make life easier for your pupils.

It will also make life easier for you.

If you communicate your boundaries clearly, then any student who oversteps the mark is not in a position to mount a credible defence of their actions. You have made clear what is not acceptable. If they then participate in unacceptable behaviour you can simply refer them to your previous communication, nullifying any efforts on their part to justify what they have done wrong.

Communicate Your Consequences

05 The same applies to consequences.

If you clearly explain which consequences follow which actions then pupils will understand what will happen if their behaviour is not up to par.

As such, they will have no defence when you invoke the appropriate consequences for their actions.

For example, you may say at the beginning of term that if someone does not complete all their classwork then they will have to stay behind to finish it. Having said this, perhaps even having repeated it on a couple of occasions, no student who fails to complete their classwork is in a position to argue that they did not know they would have to stay behind.

Of course, they still won't like the idea of staying behind! But they will have to acknowledge that the consequences were made clear to them well in advance.

Police Your Boundaries

06 As we noted earlier, young people test boundaries. We should expect them to do this and not be surprised when it happens.

Knowing this, we should also be extra vigilant in policing the boundaries we set. The reasons are threefold.

First, if we do not police the boundaries we set then we are sending out a message that they are not really that important. Paying attention to something is an indication that it matters.

Second, failing to police your boundaries will result in students realising they can push things further. If they break the boundary and nothing happens, why shouldn't they try to go further?

Third, if you do not maintain the integrity of your boundaries from the beginning it will be much harder to restore this later on.

It is a matter of consistency over time. We all learn from our experiences. If something happens repeatedly, we tend to expect it to happen again. Therefore, you should aim to ensure you police your boundaries from the very beginning.

Always Follow Through on Your Consequences

07 In a similar vein to the previous entry, make sure you always follow through on your consequences. This is especially important at the beginning of the year, or when you are picking up a new class.

If you don't follow through on your consequences then they are not consequences. A consequence only becomes real when it is enacted. Otherwise it is nothing more than an idea, ephemeral and without meaning.

If you follow through on some consequences and not on others you will find yourself being inconsistent. This is bad. Students will pick up on it and use it against you (rightly so!). They will say things like: 'Why are you punishing me when you let her get away with it?'

Inconsistency of consequences goes against our basic conception of fairness. It riles and, as a result, creates ill-feeling (and sometimes conflict).

With that said, we all miss things in the classroom. In such situations, I have found it useful to say something along the lines of: "I'm like a referee. I do my best to see everything. Sometimes I miss things, but there is no intention to do so. I can only deal with what I see, but I can't let anything I see slip by."

Don't Fold

08 There are many moments when it is tempting to fold. Perhaps we just want to leave a negative situation. Maybe we feel it isn't worth the energy. Or perhaps it's just one of those days.

Resist the temptation.

Children are brilliant negotiators. This is because they understand that, ultimately, we want to help them and won't give up on them. As such, they have the upper hand, knowing that do not have a best alternative to no agreement.

However, we can overcome this imbalance by remaining firm in the face of requests to give in.

Not folding ensures you are sending out the message that your boundaries and your consequences are important. It illustrates their certainty and the fact that they are there for a reason.

While it is important not to fold, do make sure that in so doing you don't become embroiled in conflict or in a stand-off. Should a student continue to refuse to acquiesce, ask them to leave the room, call a member of staff for support or explain that you will defer the matter until later, when you will deal with it appropriately.

Short-Term Pain = Long-Term Gain

09 So, if we could sum up the last seven entries, it would be this:

Short-term pain = long-term gain.

Initially, when working with a new class or when beginning a school year with a class you already know, it is likely that you will have moments which are difficult, testing or mildly uncomfortable.

This is an inevitable result of you setting out your boundaries and then ensuring students come to accept these.

But any short-term pain will be hugely offset by the long-term gains which result. Keep this in mind if the going gets tough. You can always conjure up an image of what your lessons would be like if you let things slide from the beginning. This should be enough to help you persist in the face of any adversity.

Be Consistent. Always.

10 I mentioned this earlier (in entry seven) but it is sufficiently important as to deserve its own entry.

Consistency is an absolutely vital part of behaviour management.

It means that pupils know what to expect.

It means that students become habituated to how you do things.

It means that your classroom is predictable (making it easier for pupils to get on and learn).

So aim to maintain consistency at all times. Behaviour management will be much simpler as a result.

Radiate Enthusiasm

11 People are infectious. We infect each other with our emotions and feelings. This happens to varying degrees but tends to be the case in many situations. Think of a time when someone made you laugh – how did it make you feel? Now think of a time when somebody lashed out at you verbally – what effect did this have?

Working from this premise – that we can influence each other through emotions and feelings – you can see why it pays to radiate enthusiasm in the classroom.

An enthusiastic teacher is far more likely to elicit good behaviour from their students than an unenthusiastic one. We all like to be around enthusiasm. It's positive; it's good; it makes us feel like things are on the up.

Students are just like the rest of us – they tend to respond well to enthusiasm.

Keep Positive

12 The same is true of positivity. Positive people lift us up. When we feel down we listen to an upbeat song to change our mood. If someone smiles at us we smile back...and smiling releases dopamine and serotonin, two chemicals which make us feel good.

By keeping positive you will be doing two things.

First, you will be making your students feel good, binding them into the lesson and the learning.

Second, you will be keeping your own morale up, making it more likely that you will teach and manage behaviour effectively.

Not all pupils will respond directly to you being positive, but few, if any, will respond negatively, making staying positive a no-lose strategy.

Praise

13 This entry and the following seven are all devoted praise. This in itself signifies the importance of the concept (and the act) to perfecting behaviour management.

Praise is great.

When someone praises us, we feel good. It shows us that what we are doing is the right thing. It is an act of acknowledgment; one which indicates that we have been noticed and that other people think what we are doing is important and worthy of attention.

It often amazes me how some teachers can go through whole lessons without praising anything. And they want students to learn, enjoy school and feel motivated!

If you doubt the efficacy of praise, simply consider how you feel when someone takes the time to tell you that you are appreciated and that what you do is good – whether this is at work or in your personal life.

In fact, let me do it for you now. You're doing a good job and you're working hard to be a better teacher. I know this because you bought this book. So thank you and keep up the good work.

Praise Spotting

14 Some students go through their school lives rarely receiving any praise. Perhaps they are quiet or shy. Perhaps they are labelled as being naughty. Perhaps they are always getting noticed for the wrong reasons.

These children need praise as much as anybody else – maybe even more so.

You can give it to them.

Make a point of identifying things for which you can praise pupils. Set out with the intention of finding opportunities to praise students, particularly those who regularly fall under the radar or attract negative attention.

Over time this process will make those pupils feel better about learning, about your lessons and about their interactions with you. The overall effect of this on behaviour in your classes will be enormous.

Genuine Praise

15 For praise to have an effect it must be genuine.

It's no good trying to give out fake praise just for the sake of it. Students will spot it a mile off.

Yet, genuine praise doesn't have to be reserved for terribly impressive feats or outstanding achievements.

Genuine praise is anything which is genuinely relevant within the context of which the praise is being given.

For example, if a pupil has spent three weeks not doing any work in your lessons and then they complete an activity, it is genuine praise to say to them: "Well done for putting the effort in to get on board with the learning today and complete the activity. I'm really pleased you've had a go."

At the same time, it would not be genuine to say: "Well done, that's brilliant! First activity completed. Fantastic! What an achievement. You're on your way now! Keep going!"

Even if the latter is well meant, it is not responding genuinely to the situation and the pupil. This will decrease the efficacy of the praise, blunting its effect.

Specific Praise

16 A simple way to make sure your praise is both *meant* genuinely and *perceived* as being genuine is to ensure that it is always specific.

Specific praise focuses on something. It avoids generalities. Therefore, it conveys the sense that you have thought carefully about the matter in hand before making an appropriate comment.

Here are two examples to illustrate the difference:

- "Well done Gemma, what a great piece of work."

- "Gemma, I think it's really interesting how you chose to start your work with a quote rather than just begin with your own thoughts. Well done for thinking creatively about the introduction."

Praise Effort, Application and Persistence

17 Whatever you praise, you will be indicating to students that this is good and that they should repeat it.

If you praise effort, application and persistence, you will help to cultivate these habits in your students.

Each of these is a worthy virtue. If your pupils come to possess all three, behaviour management will be a cinch. This is because your students will be regulating their own learning, working hard and not giving up when faced with difficulties.

Written Praise

18 You can provide praise in three ways and this is the first.

Written praise covers that which you write on student work or in student books. It is praise which will remain fixed over time. Pupils will be able to refer to it again and again.

With written praise you can highlight specific things students have done well and which you want them to remember. In addition, you can give comments which are reflective and closely connected to specific pieces of work – this is not always possible in other cases.

The final point to note is that written praise gives you a different way to communicate with pupils who may be shy, quiet or reluctant to talk in front of the whole class.

Spoken Praise

19 Spoken praise is the most common form of praise we use in the classroom. Do not stint on it.

Regularly praising the work students do, their effort, persistence and application, will create a positive atmosphere in your classroom.

Through spoken praise you can initiate positive interactions with pupils, model the behaviour and habits you would like from all your students, and start up conversations which explore the work pupils have done.

Don't forget that spoken praise can focus on individuals, pairs, groups and the whole class.

I find it particularly useful to praise the whole class at the end of a lesson if they have done well during the course of that lesson. This ensures everybody leaves feeling positive and also allows me to convey my genuine delight at their efforts.

Non-Verbal Praise

20 Non-verbal praise is the method with which most teachers are least familiar.

It involves things such as smiling, nodding your head, giving a thumbs up and other such gestures.

You can use all of these to signal to students that you are happy with what they are doing and to indicate that what they are doing is good.

One of the benefits of non-verbal praise is that it is subtle. You do not necessarily have to draw attention while doing it, nor interrupt the flow of the lesson.

You can give non-verbal praise from the front of the class or you can give it out while circulating through the room.

Plan Great Lessons

21 Having considered praise over the previous few entries, we will now move to look at lesson planning.

This is an integral part of effective behaviour management.

Great lessons engage and motivate students. They focus on learning, they challenge all pupils and they help everybody to make good progress. They are pitched so as to take account of the needs and abilities of one's students.

As such, well-planned lessons often alleviate the need for ninety-percent of what we know as behaviour management.

Keep It Challenging

22 Challenge is an important part of every good lesson. The level of challenge needs to be set sufficiently high so that students feel that what they are doing is worthwhile.

If lessons are too easy, pupils will disengage. They will be more likely to behave poorly as a result.

At the same time, if lessons are too hard then students may also disengage. Thus, getting the level of challenge right can be a tricky process.

It is well worth trying out a few different levels of challenge in your first few lessons with a new class so as to gauge what is right for them. This process is akin to feeling one's way in order to find a happy medium.

Find Ways to Ensure Success

23 Success breeds success. It fosters motivation and makes students feel good about themselves. It raises self-belief and creates positive associations. All of this will help to keep pupils focussed on the learning and less likely to behave in a manner we don't want.

Finding ways to ensure success means creating activities which are challenging but doable. For example, you might set up a task which is simple at first but which then becomes increasingly difficult.

Keeping the importance of success in mind while planning will help you to ensure your students regularly experience it as part of your lessons.

Especially at the Start

24 And where better to experience success than right at the start of the lesson?

Being able to do the lesson starter, being able to immediately engage with the lesson, binds pupils into the learning. It creates positive associations and avoids the opposite situation wherein students disengage because they feel they cannot do the task in hand.

A starter activity which facilitates success will nearly always get your lessons off to a great start.

Ask Yourself What the Students Will Be Doing

25 While planning your lessons, it is a good idea to ask yourself what your students will be doing at every point.

Many teachers do not ask this question. As such, they plan lessons which include periods where there is nothing for pupils to do. This vastly increases the likelihood that those students will disengage, behave poorly or fail to take part in the activities which follow.

If you are thinking from the pupils' perspective while planning, working out what they will be doing at all points of the lesson, then you will avoid such situations befalling you.

Personalise the Learning

26 Personalising the learning means matching it to the needs of your students.

If you personalise the learning then you do three distinct things.

First, you ensure the lessons you plan are pitched at a level which is appropriate for your pupils. This helps them to engage with the work and also ensures they are able to experience success.

Second, you avoid situations where there is a disconnection between what your students can do and what you want them to do.

Third, your pupils come to realise that your lessons are closely matched to where they are at and what they can do. While they may not be able to vocalise this fact, they will nonetheless appreciate it implicitly through the connotations they develop in relation to your teaching.

Make it Relevant

27 This is not always possible. However, if you can make the learning, or at least some of it, relevant to students' lives, then you will find them more likely to be switched on and engaged.

We all like to see the relevance in things. It gives purpose and meaning to what we are doing.

Relevance does not have to be profound. It could be as prosaic as the fact that the work you are doing is relevant for the exam. Similarly, you might stress the relevance of completing the work to the maintenance of positive relationships between you and your students (which is like a meta-relevance).

If You're Bored, They're Bored

28 And if they're bored, it's more likely they will disengage and behave in a manner you don't want.

When planning your lessons – and when teaching them – ask yourself whether you are bored. If you are, could you have done things differently? Could you have made the lesson more interesting?

Alleviating boredom doesn't mean doing all the work, performing, or making every lesson a whizz-bang fun-filled set-piece.

Usually it just means getting the pace right, asking interesting questions and using engaging activities.

But Sometimes We Need to be Bored

29 Because boredom is a fact of life and we all have to learn to deal with it.

And, what's more, some things are boring but still need to be done. Like peeling potatoes or writing out a list of keywords.

So while I stressed the importance of avoiding boredom in the previous entry, don't shy away from it completely. Rather, you might like to use it tactically. Boredom can be a tool for quietening a class down or for giving greater emphasis to a subsequent activity.

Try out some different, tactical uses of boredom while still aiming to keep lessons interesting and engaging on the whole.

Give and You Shall Receive

30 We now move away from lesson planning and towards a series of techniques you can employ to help manage behaviour in your classes.

The first is based on an old adage: give and you shall receive.

By this we mean that, what you put into a class you are likely to get back. If you are positive, engaged and interested in your students, it is more likely that they will be positive, engaged and interested in turn.

Similarly, if you are off-hand, bored and negative, your pupils probably will be as well.

We All Like Something to Look Forward To

31 It gives us a sense of hope, provides a goal to work towards and gives purpose to our present efforts.

You can take advantage of these facts by giving your students things to look forward to. This will make them work harder. It will also make them more likely to behave well.

In essence, this technique is all about creating an extrinsic motivator (the thing being looked forward to) which causes students to reconceive the work they have to do in instrumental terms (it becomes an instrument through which they can reach the goal).

Furthermore, you can use whatever it is you are looking forward to in your speech. For example:

"Stay on task please; remember what we're all working towards."

Manners All Round

32 It is difficult to react negatively to someone who displays excellent manners. It is also difficult to go directly against what they ask. Furthermore, excellent manners act as a model for students to follow.

By setting the tone for how interactions are to take place in your classroom, you will be signally what is and what isn't acceptable.

Maintaining good manners at all times will send a powerful message to your pupils. After all, manners are at root a verbal and visual acknowledgement of the importance of others. They convey respect and, generally, command it as well.

Model, Model, Model

33 Everything you do in the classroom is a model for your pupils to imitate. Bearing this in mind is important.

If you want your students to behave well and to engage with the learning, model this for them. If you want them to listen carefully and speak respectfully, model this for them. If you want them to interact positively with everyone they work with, model this for them.

You can draw attention to the modelling you do, explicitly mentioning it to pupils, or you can simply let it have its effect through the drip-drip of repetition.

Never Speak if They're Speaking

34 Perhaps one of the biggest issues many teachers face in terms of behaviour management is getting the class quiet and keeping them quiet while they (the teacher) are speaking.

Following this simple rule will go a long way to dealing with such a problem.

If you want silence, wait for it. Do not be tempted to start speaking if students are still speaking. Stand at the front of the class, ask for silence and then wait.

This may feel uncomfortable at times, but persist. You need to convey the message that your expectations will be met. Over time, pupils will come to terms with this and fall to silence much more quickly.

Don't be Afraid to Wait

35 As I said in the last entry, don't be afraid to wait for silence. I reiterate this here because it can be really difficult. One feels the pressure to move on or the sensation that waiting is somehow foolish.

Steel yourself. Don't be afraid to wait.

Ultimately, it is about conveying a clear message to students. And that message is: I have asked for silence so that I can talk to everybody and move the learning on. I expect silence and I will wait for it.

Remain Flexible

36 Flexibility gives you the means to respond to situations as they arise. Throughout this book I have been stressing the virtues of consistency and the wider process of habituating students into certain ways of doing things. All the same, one shouldn't let this slip over into rigidity.

Rigidity militates against good behaviour management because it makes the rules an end in themselves instead of a means to an end. This transfers the purpose of your practice from ensuring a great learning environment to ensuring the rules are followed. There is a subtle but important difference.

Remaining flexible can help prevent situations arising in which the rules become too dominate, taking on a life of their own.

Sense the Atmosphere

37 Every lesson has an atmosphere. This is a difficult thing to describe. It is perhaps best illustrated through an example. Consider how you felt on an occasion when you went into someone else's lesson. What did you pick up? What did you sense? That was the atmosphere.

Sensing the atmosphere in your own lessons means attending closely to how pupils are interacting, observing what sort of emotions are swirling around, and analysing the body language in the room.

The information you elicit – which provides you with a sense of the atmosphere – can then be used to adapt your teaching for the purposes of successful behaviour management. For example, if you sense the atmosphere is loose and unstructured, you might introduce a focussed, independent writing activity you had not previously intended to use.

Focus on the Small Things

38 Because, if you focus on these, the big things won't even enter the picture.

But Don't Get Pedantic

39 Because if you do, the atmosphere will sour. Focus on the small things but do so in an upbeat and positive way which still brooks no compromise or dissension.

High Standards

40 Pupils will very quickly pick up on your expectations. They will know after the first couple of lessons what you are prepared to accept and what you will let slide. Within a short period of time they will have come to understand and internalise your standards.

So set high standards. As high as possible.

Don't worry if they are so high they are unlikely to be met. They can still act as an ideal towards which you and your class are always working.

And remember, it is far easier to start off with high standards and then lower these slightly than it is to start off with low standards which you then try to raise up.

Lock-Down Lessons

41 A lock-down lesson is a lesson you have ready and prepared for those classes who, for whatever reason, are struggling to work successfully; classes whose behaviour is not coming up to par.

Such lessons are ones in which there is almost no opportunity for pupils to behave poorly. For example, an hour-long lesson in which students have to read a text, write about the text, read a second text, write about this, and then produce their own text. In this example, all pupils have clear instructions, more than enough work to cover the whole lesson and, crucially, it is work which is independent and needs to be completed in silence.

These types of lessons are brilliant if you want to regain control over a class or reassert the importance of excellent behaviour. Come up with a few and have them ready to hand for whenever the need arises.

Use Your Seating Plan

42 Your seating plan is a powerful behaviour management tool. One of the key causes of behavioural issues in the classroom is interactions between particular students – often ones who are friends outside lessons and who bring their social behaviour into the classroom.

By carefully planning where pupils will sit you can minimise the opportunity for off-topic conversations and off-task behaviour.

In addition, you can sit students who need more support near to you or in places which are easy for you to access. This will allow you to give these pupils more of your time, thus helping them to engage successfully with the learning (and therefore decreasing the chance that they will let their behaviour slide).

Say 'Thanks'

43 This is a simple technique you can use to gain acquiescence to instructions. It works as follows:

Instead of saying: "Can you sit down quietly, please."

Say: "Can you sit down quietly, thanks."

In the second case, you are implicitly suggesting that the instruction has already been agreed to. This removes the sense that you are asking without the statement transforming into an order, which can come across as rude and which can easily engender conflict.

Take Control

44 Beyond anything else, perfect behaviour management comes down to you taking control of the classroom, the learning and the lesson.

This is a theme which has run throughout the book. Early on we talked about taking control of your planning, then of the atmosphere (through giving praise), the expectations and the norms which constitute your lessons.

Being alive to the notion of control in the classroom allows you to reflect on whether or not you are in charge of things and whether you are using your position and your authority to manage the learning successfully. Ask yourself at each stage of the teaching process whether you are in control or not. If the answer is no, ask yourself what you could do to change things.

Eventually, when your students are well-trained, familiar with your expectations and possessed of good relationships to you, control will become less of an issue. Prior to this point, however, you should pay it close attention.

Organisation is Key

45 If you are organised then you can deal effectively with situations which arise. This is because you will be able to give your full attention to what is in front of you.

If you are disorganised, your attention will be divided between what you are trying to do and what is going on around you.

In addition, disorganisation promotes poor behaviour because it slows the pace of lessons, cedes control of the learning and sends out the message that students do not need to take the lesson that seriously.

Use Your Voice

46 There are many different ways you can use your voice to aid behaviour management. Here are five examples:

- Speak slowly and calmly so as to dampen the energy levels of a lively class.

- Inject drama into your voice when introducing an activity so as to increase motivation and engagement.

- Raise your voice (but always try to avoid shouting) to signal that certain behaviour is unacceptable.

- When the whole class is silent, speak quietly to really focus attention onto your words.

- Project your voice confidently in order to convey your authority.

Use Your Body

47 You can also use your body to aid behaviour management. Here are five simple techniques:

- Circulate around the room during activities. This way you can check that everyone is on task.

- If a student is off-task during an activity, stand next to them. Often this alone is enough to alter their behaviour.

- Try teaching from the back of the class to see the different effect it has on students.

- Wear smart, professional clothes to convey an air of authority and seriousness.

- Use calming hand gestures to dampen a highly-charged atmosphere (such as holding your hands up with open palms or slowly lowering both hands as if closing a car boot).

Never Break a Silence

48 If your class are working in silence, don't break that silence. Let it grow and take over the room. Leave pupils to focus on their work. If you break the silence, it will be hard to get back. Students will see that you have broken it and believe, whether consciously or not, that it is alright for them to do the same.

So don't break the silence.

Do Your Research

49 If you are taking a new class, do your research. Find out about the pupils in that class. Use this information to help inform your seating plan and your lesson planning.

If you have a student who is behaving particularly poorly in your lessons, do your research. Find out how they behave in other lessons. See if other teachers have found strategies which work with them.

If you have a class who prove particularly challenging to teach, do your research. Maybe other teachers are finding the same thing and this is a wider issue to which senior management need to be alerted. Or perhaps a colleague will be able to give you advice on how to turn things around.

Stay Calm

50 And so we conclude our tour of 50 quick ways to perfect behaviour management by emphasising the importance of staying calm.

If we are calm, we make better decisions.

If we are calm, we avoid being led by emotions – and don't forget the classroom can be an emotional place.

If we are calm, we are in a better position to achieve our long-term goals because we make choices based on reason and evidence rather than emotion.

And think of the different messages conveyed to students by two teachers, one who loses their temper in the face of poor behaviour and one who remains calm. The latter will always achieve better results over time. They will teach a better lesson as well, in more ways than one.

A Brief Request

If you have found this book useful I would be delighted if you could leave a review on Amazon to let others know.

If you have any thoughts or comments, or if you have an idea for a new book in the series you would like me to write, please don't hesitate to get in touch at mike@mikegershon.com.

Finally, don't forget that you can download all my teaching and learning resources for **FREE** at www.mikegershon.com.

CPSIA information can be obtained
at www.ICGtesting.com
Printed in the USA
LVOW04s0913130816
500247LV00020B/923/P

9 781508 540199